Anti-inflammatory Diet Cookbook

Simple Anti-Inflammatory Cookbook with 5-Ingredient Recipes and a 21-Day Reset Plan to Heal the Gut, Balance Hormones, Ease Arthritis, and Restore All-Day Energy

Abigail Douglas

Table of Contents

Anti-inflammatory Diet Cookbook 1

Preface 13

Chapter 1 17

    Understanding Inflammation 17

        Acute vs. Chronic Inflammation 18

    The Joints: Where Pain Speaks Loudest 19

    The Gut: Inflammation's Hidden Gateway 19

    Hormones: The Silent Messengers 20

    Why Food is the Frontline Defense 21

    A Gentle Beginning 22

Chapter 2 24

The Anti-Inflammatory Pantry 24

Core Staples: Spices, Herbs, Oils, and Whole Foods 24

    Spices & Herbs: 25

    Oils & Healthy Fats: 25

    Whole Foods: 26

Foods to Avoid: The Inflammation Triggers 27

Smart Shopping & Label Reading 28

A Kitchen That Heals 30

Chapter 3 32

The 5-Ingredient Simplicity Method 32

Why Fewer Ingredients = Less Stress & More Healing
.... 33

Cooking Tips for Busy Lives 34

How to Swap Ingredients Easily (Vegan, Gluten-Free, and Beyond) 35

A Simpler Way to Heal 36

Chapter 4 38

The 21-Day Reset Plan 38

Phase 1: Calm Inflammation (Week 1) 39

Phase 2: Heal the Gut & Balance Hormones (Week 2) 40

Phase 3: Energy Restoration (Week 3) 41

Daily Structure: Your Reset Framework 42

Your Invitation to Reset 43

Chapter 5 45

  Energizing Breakfasts 45

    Smoothies: A Glass of Healing Power 46

    Oats: Comfort in a Bowl 47

    Scrambles & Frittatas: Protein for Stability 47

    Anti-Inflammatory Morning Tonics 48

    Make-Ahead Ideas for Busy Mornings 49

  The Energy Advantage 50

Chapter 6 52

  Healing Lunches 52

    Salads: More Than Just Lettuce 53

    Wraps: Portable Healing Meals 54

Soups: Comfort in a Bowl 55

Meal-Prep Bowls: Your Weekly Ally 55

Light but Sustaining Meals 56

Flavor Balancing: Sweet, Savory, Tangy 57

Lunch as a Healing Pause 58

Chapter 7 60

Restorative Dinners 60

One-Pan Meals: Simplicity Meets Healing 61

Baked Salmon: A Healing Classic 62

Veggie Stir-Fries: Fast & Flavorful 63

Comfort Classics Reimagined 63

Family-Friendly Twists 64

The Power of Evening Nourishment 65

Chapter 8 67

Snacks & Small Bites... 67

Quick Energy Balls 68

Veggie Sticks & Dips... 68

Smart Swaps for Chips & Cookies 69

Evening Snacks That Don't Spike Inflammation 70

The Joy of Small Bites 71

Chapter 9 73

Sweet Healing Treats 73

Low-Sugar, Gut-Friendly Desserts 73

Chia Puddings: Small Seeds, Big Healing............. 74

Baked Apples: Nature's Comfort Dessert 75

Dark Chocolate Recipes: A Sweet Antioxidant Boost 76

Tips for Satisfying Sweet Cravings 78

The Sweet Side of Healing 79

Chapter 10 81

Drinks & Tonics 81

Herbal Teas: Nature's Gentle Healers 81

Golden Milk: A Cup of Liquid Sunshine 83

Anti-Inflammatory Smoothies 83

Electrolyte Water Blends... 84

Drinks for Digestion and Energy 85

The Healing Power of Sipping 86

Chapter 11 88

Lifestyle Beyond the Plate 88

Stress Reduction: The Hidden Key 88

Gentle Movement & Inflammation 90

Creating a Sustainable Anti-Inflammatory Lifestyle . 91

The Bigger Picture 92

21-Day Anti-Inflammatory Meal Plan (Printable Companion) 97

Week 1 – Calm Inflammation 97

Week 2 – Heal the Gut & Balance Hormones 101

Week 3 – Energy Restoration 104

Acknowledgment 108

Copyright © 2025 by Abigail Douglas

All rights reserved. No part of this book may be copied, reproduced, stored, or transmitted in any form or by any means—electronic, mechanical, photocopying, recording, or otherwise without prior written permission from the publisher, except for brief quotations used in reviews or scholarly works.

Disclaimer

This book is for educational and informational purposes only and is not intended as medical advice. Always consult with a qualified healthcare professional before making any dietary, lifestyle, or supplement changes, especially if you have existing health conditions or are taking medications. The author and publisher disclaim responsibility for any adverse effects that may result from the use of information presented herein.

Preface

When I first began exploring the connection between food and health, one truth stood out above all others: inflammation is at the root of so many of the struggles people face every single day. From stiff joints and bloating to stubborn belly fat, low energy, and hormone imbalances, chronic inflammation quietly affects millions. And yet, with the right foods and daily habits, healing is possible—not through deprivation, but through nourishment.

This cookbook was born out of a desire to make that healing journey simple, delicious, and realistic for everyday life. Too often, diets feel overwhelming with complicated recipes, long ingredient lists, and rigid rules. That's why I built this book around 5-ingredient recipes and a structured 21-day anti-inflammatory reset plan. My goal is to give you more than recipes—I want to hand you a roadmap for lasting energy, easier digestion, calmer joints, and renewed vitality.

Inside these pages, you'll discover:

- **Quick & easy anti-inflammatory meals** that work for busy mornings, lunches on the go, and comforting dinners.
- **5-ingredient recipes** that remove the stress from cooking while still delivering powerful healing benefits.
- A step-by-step **21-day anti-inflammatory meal plan** designed to calm inflammation, heal the gut, balance hormones, and restore all-day energy.
- **Smart swaps** for snacks, treats, and drinks so you never feel deprived while supporting joint health, digestion, and weight management.

You don't need to be a chef to succeed with this plan. You don't even need hours in the kitchen. With simple recipes, nourishing ingredients, and a practical structure, you'll discover how easy it can be to follow an **anti-inflammatory diet**—one that helps reduce arthritis pain, supports weight loss, balances hormones, and boosts energy naturally.

This isn't just a cookbook—it's a lifestyle companion. Every recipe, every tip, and every meal plan has been designed to help you feel lighter, clearer, and more energized. Whether your goal is to find relief from inflammation-related symptoms, improve digestion, lose stubborn weight, or simply support your body with healing foods, you'll find everything you need here.

Food can be your most powerful medicine. And with the recipes and strategies in this book, I hope you'll experience firsthand how small, daily choices can lead to lasting transformation.

Here's to restoring your health—one delicious, healing

bite at a time.

Chapter 1

Understanding Inflammation

If you've ever twisted an ankle, burned your hand on the stove, or caught the flu, you've experienced inflammation at work. The swelling, redness, heat, and tenderness are all signs that your body's defense system has rushed in to protect you. In that sense, inflammation is not your enemy—it's one of the most powerful healing responses you have.

The problem arises when this short-term healing mechanism turns into a long-term fire that never goes out. Instead of switching off once the danger has passed, the body remains on high alert. This is what we call chronic inflammation, and it quietly fuels some of the most common struggles people face today: achy joints, stubborn belly fat, sluggish digestion, brain fog, hormonal imbalances, and low energy that no amount of coffee can fix.

Acute vs. Chronic Inflammation

Think of acute inflammation as an emergency response team. You cut your finger, and within moments, white blood cells arrive, swelling begins, and the area turns warm and red. This is the body's way of disinfecting, repairing, and protecting. Within days, the injury heals and the inflammation subsides.

Chronic inflammation, however, is like a smoke alarm that won't stop blaring even after the fire is out. Instead of helping, it becomes harmful. Persistent inflammation can damage tissues, wear down cartilage, interfere with hormones, and disrupt the immune system. It is now widely recognized as a root cause or contributing factor in conditions like arthritis, diabetes, heart disease, irritable bowel syndrome, depression, and even some cancers.

The Joints: Where Pain Speaks Loudest

When inflammation lingers in the joints, it shows up as stiffness, swelling, and pain. Conditions like osteoarthritis and rheumatoid arthritis are classic examples. Everyday tasks—opening a jar, climbing stairs, even holding a pen—can feel like a struggle. Many people turn to painkillers or anti-inflammatory drugs for relief, but food can be a gentler and more sustainable ally.

The Gut: Inflammation's Hidden Gateway

Scientists often call the gut the "second brain," and for good reason. About 70% of your immune system lives in your gut lining. When inflammation damages this delicate system, it can lead to digestive distress, food sensitivities, leaky gut, and a cascade of immune-related issues. The gut is often the starting point for healing, and what we eat either restores balance or fans the flames.

Hormones: The Silent Messengers

Your hormones are chemical messengers that regulate everything from mood and sleep to metabolism and weight. Chronic inflammation can interfere with hormone production and signaling. For women, this may look like irregular cycles, hot flashes, or difficulty losing weight. For both men and women, it often shows up as stubborn belly fat, low energy, or disrupted sleep patterns. Healing inflammation helps restore hormonal balance naturally, without relying on quick fixes.

Energy: From Burnout to Renewal

If you wake up tired no matter how long you sleep, or if you experience that mid-afternoon crash daily, chronic inflammation could be draining your energy reserves. The body expends enormous effort trying to put out internal fires. Once you begin eating in a way that lowers inflammation, many people are astonished to discover how quickly their energy levels rebound. It feels as if someone has turned the lights back on inside.

Why Food is the Frontline Defense

Every bite you take is either fighting inflammation or feeding it. Sugary drinks, refined carbs, processed oils, and packaged snacks create a fertile ground for inflammation. On the other hand, whole foods rich in antioxidants, healthy fats, fiber, and phytonutrients act like a natural fire extinguisher.

Turmeric and ginger help calm swollen joints. Omega-3s from salmon and chia seeds soothe cellular inflammation. Leafy greens and berries provide antioxidants that neutralize free radicals. Olive oil, nuts, and seeds deliver anti-inflammatory fats that nourish instead of harm.

The beauty of this truth is empowering: you don't have to live at the mercy of inflammation. You can influence it every single day with the meals you prepare and the foods you choose.

A Gentle Beginning

This book is not about restriction, deprivation, or rigid rules. It's about discovering foods that taste wonderful, are easy to prepare, and quietly work behind the scenes to restore balance in your body. By the end of this journey, you'll not only understand inflammation—you'll know how to soothe it, prevent it, and keep your body thriving for years to come.

So as we step into the recipes and the 21-Day Reset, keep this in mind: inflammation may be powerful, but food is even more powerful. And when chosen wisely, it can be your most loyal medicine.

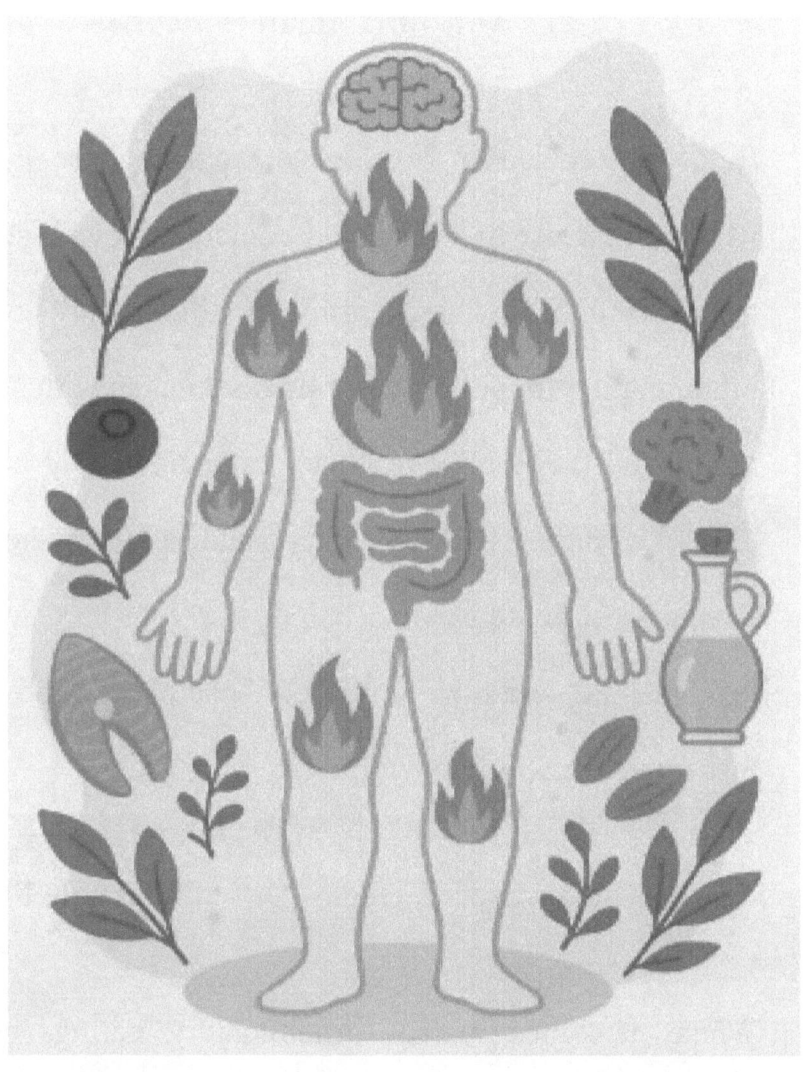

Chapter 2

The Anti-Inflammatory Pantry

Before you cook a single recipe, the real magic begins with what you choose to keep on your shelves. A well-stocked pantry is like having an army of allies ready to fight inflammation for you. If you fill your kitchen with healing foods, you'll naturally reach for ingredients that nourish instead of harm. Think of this chapter as your shopping compass—a guide to what belongs in your cart, what to leave behind, and how to decode those tricky food labels that try to sneak inflammation into your diet.

Core Staples: Spices, Herbs, Oils, and Whole Foods

When it comes to anti-inflammatory eating, certain ingredients stand out as everyday heroes. You'll see them woven throughout the recipes in this book because they are both flavorful and medicinal.

Spices & Herbs:

- Turmeric – golden root rich in curcumin, known for calming joint inflammation.
- Ginger – warms digestion and soothes nausea.
- Cinnamon – balances blood sugar and reduces inflammation.
- Garlic & Onions – natural antimicrobials that strengthen immunity.
- Rosemary, Oregano, Basil, Thyme – herbs packed with antioxidants that also make meals taste alive.

Oils & Healthy Fats:

- Extra-Virgin Olive Oil – the backbone of Mediterranean anti-inflammatory eating.

- Avocados & Avocado Oil – creamy, nourishing, and heart-friendly.
- Coconut Oil (unrefined) – supports gut health and stable energy.
- Nuts & Seeds (almonds, walnuts, chia, flax) – tiny but powerful carriers of omega-3s.

Whole Foods:

- Fatty fish (salmon, sardines, mackerel) – reduce cellular inflammation.
- Leafy greens (spinach, kale, arugula) – flood the body with antioxidants.
- Colorful vegetables (broccoli, bell peppers, beets) – each color signals unique plant compounds that fight free radicals.
- Legumes & lentils – high in fiber, gentle on blood sugar.

- Berries & fruits (blueberries, cherries, citrus) – natural anti-inflammatory sweeteners from nature.

Foods to Avoid: The Inflammation Triggers

Just as important as what you add is what you leave behind. Some foods quietly stoke the fire of inflammation, often without us realizing it. By reducing or eliminating these, you give your body room to heal.

- Refined sugars: Candy, sodas, sweetened cereals, pastries. These spike blood sugar, triggering insulin and inflammatory pathways.
- Processed oils: Corn oil, soybean oil, canola oil, and anything labeled "hydrogenated." These are rich in omega-6 fats that, when out of balance, fuel inflammation.

- Refined carbohydrates: White bread, pasta, crackers, and white rice—stripped of fiber and nutrients, they act like sugar in the body.

- Highly processed snacks: Chips, cookies, frozen meals, deli meats, and fast food. Convenience comes at the cost of hidden additives, sodium, and preservatives that burden your system.

- Excess alcohol: A glass of red wine may have antioxidants, but excess drinking irritates the gut and liver, both central to inflammation control.

Smart Shopping & Label Reading

The grocery store can be tricky—bright packaging and "healthy" claims often mask foods that keep you inflamed. Here's how to shop smarter:

- **Go around the perimeter first.** Fresh produce, meats, and whole foods are usually along the outer aisles. The middle aisles are where processed traps hide.

- **Read ingredient lists, not just labels.** If a food has more than five ingredients, or if you can't pronounce half of them, it probably doesn't belong in your anti-inflammatory kitchen.
- **Watch for hidden sugars.** They appear under many names: sucrose, fructose, corn syrup, maltose, agave nectar, and more.
- **Check the oils.** If you see "partially hydrogenated" or cheap oils like soybean or corn, put it back.
- **Choose whole over refined.** Brown rice instead of white, whole oats instead of instant, whole fruit instead of fruit juice.

Shopping this way may feel different at first, but it quickly becomes second nature. Over time, you'll walk through the store with confidence, knowing exactly which foods are building health instead of tearing it down.

A Kitchen That Heals

Your pantry sets the tone for your healing journey. When you open your cupboard and see jars of nuts, shelves of olive oil and spices, and baskets of colorful vegetables, it feels inviting instead of overwhelming. Remember, the kitchen is more than a place to cook—it's your pharmacy, your laboratory, and your sanctuary.

Every choice you make here lays the foundation for less pain, more energy, and a life where inflammation no longer controls you.

Chapter 3

The 5-Ingredient Simplicity Method

One of the most common obstacles people face when trying to eat healthier is the belief that it's complicated. Long ingredient lists, unfamiliar spices, and elaborate techniques can feel overwhelming—especially on busy weeknights. That's why this book embraces the 5-Ingredient Simplicity Method: meals built from just a handful of powerful foods that heal, energize, and taste incredible.

This isn't about restriction. It's about stripping cooking back to what matters most: flavor, nourishment, and ease. When you cook with fewer ingredients, you spend less time chopping, cleaning, and second-guessing recipes. More importantly, you reduce stress in the kitchen, which translates into less stress on your body. And since stress itself is a form of inflammation, simplifying your meals is not just practical—it's healing.

Why Fewer Ingredients = Less Stress & More Healing

Cooking with 20 different ingredients doesn't automatically make a dish healthier. In fact, the more processed items you add, the more likely hidden sugars, preservatives, or oils sneak in.

By focusing on **just five whole ingredients**, you:

- Reduce exposure to additives and chemicals.
- Allow the natural healing power of food to shine.
- Make it easier to stay consistent with your anti-inflammatory lifestyle.
- Spend less money at the grocery store, since your meals rely on multipurpose staples.

Think of it as decluttering your plate. When your body doesn't have to battle extra toxins, it can focus its energy on repairing tissues, balancing hormones, and calming inflammation.

Cooking Tips for Busy Lives

Eating anti-inflammatory doesn't mean spending hours in the kitchen. In fact, with smart strategies, you can prepare meals faster than ordering takeout.

- **Batch cook smart proteins.** Roast a tray of salmon fillets, chicken breasts, or lentils on Sunday. Reheat them throughout the week with different spices and sides.
- **Use one-pan methods.** Sheet-pan dinners, skillet stir-fries, and Instant Pot soups minimize cleanup.
- **Lean on freezer heroes.** Frozen spinach, berries, or broccoli are just as nutrient-rich as fresh and save chopping time.

- **Prep once, eat twice.** Cook extra portions of grains, soups, or dressings to carry into lunches or dinners the next day.
- **Keep flavor boosters ready.** Lemon wedges, olive oil, fresh herbs, and garlic can transform even the simplest dish.

The secret isn't to spend more time cooking—it's to cook smarter with what you already have.

How to Swap Ingredients Easily (Vegan, Gluten-Free, and Beyond)

One of the joys of the 5-Ingredient Simplicity Method is flexibility. These recipes are designed to adapt to your preferences and dietary needs. If you don't eat dairy, gluten, or meat, you'll still find endless options.

- **Protein swaps:** Replace chicken with chickpeas, salmon with tofu, or beef with lentils.

- **Grain swaps:** Use quinoa, cauliflower rice, or sweet potatoes instead of wheat pasta or bread.
- **Dairy swaps:** Choose almond milk, coconut yogurt, or cashew cream instead of cow's milk or cheese.
- **Flavor swaps:** Don't have rosemary? Use thyme or oregano. Out of olive oil? Avocado oil works beautifully.

Think of recipes as flexible formulas, not rigid instructions. The goal is to empower you, not trap you. Once you learn a handful of base techniques, you can play with endless variations using what's fresh, affordable, and available in your kitchen.

A Simpler Way to Heal

Food should never feel like another chore on your to-do list. By embracing the 5-Ingredient Simplicity Method, you're not just cooking—you're creating space for healing in your everyday life. You'll notice meals becoming less stressful, more enjoyable, and surprisingly delicious. Simplicity, after all, is often the ultimate sophistication.

37

Chapter 4

The 21-Day Reset Plan

Change doesn't happen overnight. Healing your body from chronic inflammation is a journey—one that becomes far less overwhelming when broken down into manageable steps. That's the power of the **21-Day Reset Plan**: a focused, three-week roadmap that teaches your body to calm inflammation, restore balance, and renew energy.

By committing just three weeks, you give yourself the chance to feel what life is like without the constant weight of inflammation. Many readers report lighter joints, clearer digestion, improved moods, and a surge of vitality they thought was lost. This reset isn't about restriction—it's about nourishment, structure, and support.

Phase 1: Calm Inflammation (Week 1)

The first week is all about *quieting the fire*. Think of it as telling your body, "It's safe now." During this phase, you'll gently remove the most common inflammatory triggers—refined sugar, processed oils, and packaged foods—while flooding your system with healing nutrients.

- **Focus foods:** Leafy greens, fatty fish (salmon, sardines), turmeric, ginger, berries, nuts, olive oil.
- **What to avoid:** Soda, pastries, fried foods, processed meats, excess caffeine.
- **Lifestyle support:** Aim for 7–8 hours of sleep, light stretching or walks daily, and deep breathing exercises to reduce stress.

By the end of Week 1, many notice reduced bloating, steadier energy, and less joint stiffness.

Phase 2: Heal the Gut & Balance Hormones (Week 2)

Now that inflammation is settling, it's time to focus on the gut—the command center of your immune system—and the delicate balance of hormones that regulate mood, weight, and energy.

- **Focus foods:** Probiotic-rich yogurt (or coconut yogurt), sauerkraut, kefir, bone broth, fiber-rich vegetables, flaxseed, chia seeds.
- **What to avoid:** Artificial sweeteners, alcohol, excess gluten or dairy (unless well tolerated).
- **Lifestyle support:** Gentle core exercises for digestion, daily hydration with herbal teas, and consistent mealtimes to stabilize blood sugar and hormones.

By the end of Week 2, expect easier digestion, more balanced moods, and fewer food cravings.

Phase 3: Energy Restoration (Week 3)

The final week is about building resilience and unlocking energy. With inflammation calmed and the gut supported, your body is ready to thrive. This is when many feel their "lights come back on."

- **Focus foods:** Balanced meals combining clean protein, healthy fats, and slow-digesting carbs (quinoa, sweet potatoes, lentils). Citrus fruits and green smoothies for vibrancy.
- **What to avoid:** Late-night snacking, overly processed "energy" drinks or bars.

- Lifestyle support: Add joyful movement—yoga, dancing, brisk walks. Prioritize morning hydration and an evening wind-down ritual.

By the end of Week 3, energy levels often soar, mental clarity sharpens, and the foundation for a long-term anti-inflammatory lifestyle is set.

Daily Structure: Your Reset Framework

To make this plan effortless, here's the simple daily rhythm to follow throughout the 21 days:

1. **Meals:** Three balanced meals + one healing snack if needed. Each meal pairs lean protein, healthy fats, colorful vegetables, and anti-inflammatory spices.
2. **Hydration:** Begin your morning with warm lemon water or an herbal tonic. Aim for at least 8 glasses of water or herbal tea daily.

3. **Movement:** Gentle exercise—20–30 minutes of walking, yoga, or stretching. Consistency is more important than intensity.
4. **Journaling:** End your day with 5 minutes of reflection. Write down:
- What you ate.
- How your body felt (energy, digestion, pain).
- One thing you're grateful for.

This daily journaling becomes a powerful tool—it shows you patterns, celebrates progress, and keeps motivation high.

Your Invitation to Reset

These 21 days are not a punishment. They're an invitation—to discover how amazing you can feel when inflammation no longer rules your body. Remember, it's not about perfection. It's about consistency, compassion, and noticing even the smallest wins.

By the end of this reset, you'll not only feel lighter and more energized—you'll have the tools to make these habits a natural part of your lifestyle.

Chapter 5

Energizing Breakfasts

They say breakfast sets the tone for the day—and when you're healing inflammation, this couldn't be more true. The first foods you eat in the morning either fan the flames of inflammation (hello, sugary cereal and processed pastries) or extinguish them with nourishment that fuels your body and mind.

An anti-inflammatory breakfast doesn't have to be complicated. It's about pairing clean proteins, healthy fats, and colorful plants in ways that taste good and keep you satisfied until lunch. Whether you're sipping a vibrant smoothie, enjoying a hearty scramble, or pouring a quick bowl of overnight oats, these morning meals give you steady energy without the crashes.

Smoothies: A Glass of Healing Power

Smoothies are one of the simplest ways to flood your body with anti-inflammatory foods before the day gets hectic. They're quick, customizable, and portable.

- **Base ideas:** Almond milk, coconut water, or green tea.
- **Healing add-ins:** Fresh spinach, kale, blueberries, flaxseed, turmeric, or ginger.
- **Protein power:** A scoop of plant-based protein powder, Greek yogurt, or chia seeds.

Tip: Freeze pre-portioned smoothie bags with fruit and greens. In the morning, just dump into the blender, add liquid, and blend.

Oats: Comfort in a Bowl

Oats are naturally high in fiber and easy on digestion, making them a perfect breakfast base. Instead of sugary instant packets, go for rolled or steel-cut oats and dress them with anti-inflammatory toppings.

- **Anti-inflammatory toppings:** Blueberries, walnuts, pumpkin seeds, cinnamon, almond butter, chia jam.
- **Savory spin:** Top oats with sautéed spinach, avocado slices, and a drizzle of olive oil.

Tip: Make overnight oats in jars with almond milk, chia seeds, and fruit. Grab one on your way out the door.

Scrambles & Frittatas: Protein for

Stability

Eggs are a powerhouse for steady energy. Scrambles and frittatas also let you pack in anti-inflammatory vegetables first thing in the morning.

- **Veggie options:** Spinach, bell peppers, onions, zucchini, mushrooms.
- **Flavor boosts:** Garlic, turmeric, black pepper, and fresh herbs.
- **Dairy-free swaps:** Coconut milk or cashew cream instead of cheese for creaminess.

Tip: Bake a large veggie-loaded frittata on Sunday. Slice into wedges and reheat for quick weekday breakfasts.

Anti-Inflammatory Morning Tonics

Before or with breakfast, sip on a healing tonic that wakes up your body gently.

- **Golden milk:** Warm almond milk with turmeric, cinnamon, ginger, and a dash of black pepper.
- **Ginger-lemon tea:** Fresh ginger slices steeped in hot water with lemon juice.
- **Green elixir:** Matcha blended with coconut milk for calm, focused energy.

Tip: Prep spice blends in small jars for golden milk or teas so you can scoop and stir without fuss.

Make-Ahead Ideas for Busy Mornings

Life doesn't always leave time to cook a hot breakfast—but that doesn't mean you have to sacrifice nourishment.

- **Egg muffins:** Whisk eggs with spinach, onions, and herbs. Bake in muffin tins and store in the fridge.

- **Chia puddings:** Mix chia seeds with coconut milk, cinnamon, and fruit. Set overnight for a ready-to-go breakfast.
- **Energy bars:** Blend oats, almond butter, dates, and flaxseed. Cut into squares for grab-and-go fuel.

The Energy Advantage

An energizing breakfast doesn't just fill your stomach—it sets your metabolism, hormones, and mindset up for success. By starting your day with anti-inflammatory ingredients, you reduce mid-morning crashes, sharpen your focus, and strengthen your body against stressors.

When you take the time—even a few minutes—to nourish yourself in the morning, you send a powerful message to your body: *You matter, and today you'll thrive.*

Chapter 6

Healing Lunches

Lunch is often the most overlooked meal of the day. Between busy schedules, meetings, or errands, it's tempting to grab something quick and processed. But lunch is your midday reset button. A well-chosen meal can steady blood sugar, calm inflammation, and keep your energy flowing into the afternoon. Skipping it or settling for fast food often leads to that familiar 3 p.m. crash, brain fog, and cravings.

Healing lunches don't need to be heavy—they need to be **light but sustaining**, packed with nutrients, and easy to prepare ahead of time. This chapter focuses on colorful salads, hearty wraps, warming soups, and versatile meal-prep bowls that satisfy without weighing you down.

Salads: More Than Just Lettuce

Forget boring bowls of iceberg and tomatoes. An anti-inflammatory salad is vibrant, nutrient-rich, and satisfying enough to stand as a full meal. The key is balance:

- **Base:** leafy greens like spinach, kale, or arugula.
- **Protein:** grilled salmon, chickpeas, or hard-boiled eggs.
- **Healthy fats:** avocado slices, walnuts, or olive oil dressing.
- **Extras for flavor:** berries for sweetness, pumpkin seeds for crunch, roasted veggies for depth.

Tip: Mason jar salads are perfect for meal prep. Layer dressing at the bottom, then hearty vegetables, proteins, and leafy greens on top. Shake when ready to eat.

Wraps: Portable Healing Meals

Wraps make anti-inflammatory eating simple and convenient. Instead of flour tortillas, try collard greens, romaine lettuce leaves, or gluten-free wraps.

- **Mediterranean wrap:** Hummus, cucumber, roasted red peppers, olives, and arugula.
- **Salmon & avocado wrap:** Flaked salmon, avocado slices, spinach, and lemon-tahini drizzle.
- **Chickpea curry wrap:** Mashed chickpeas with turmeric, garlic, and Greek yogurt wrapped in collard greens.

Tip: For sturdier wraps, blanch large collard greens in hot water for 30 seconds—softens them without losing nutrients.

Soups: Comfort in a Bowl

A bowl of soup can be one of the most soothing lunches—warm, hydrating, and deeply nourishing. Soups are also excellent vehicles for anti-inflammatory spices.

- **Healing bone broth:** Simmer with garlic, turmeric, ginger, and vegetables.
- **Lentil & spinach soup:** Packed with protein, fiber, and leafy greens.
- **Roasted tomato & basil soup:** A simple comfort classic, made without heavy cream.

Tip: Make a big pot on Sunday. Store individual servings in jars or freezer containers for quick heat-and-eat lunches.

Meal-Prep Bowls: Your Weekly Ally

Bowls are the ultimate flexible lunch. Think of them as nutrient blueprints: grain + protein + vegetables + sauce.

- **Base grains:** quinoa, brown rice, cauliflower rice, sweet potato cubes.
- **Protein options:** chicken breast, tofu, boiled eggs, or beans.
- **Vegetables:** roasted zucchini, bell peppers, broccoli, or leafy greens.
- **Sauces:** tahini-lemon, avocado crema, olive oil-herb, or miso-ginger.

Tip: Prep 3–4 bowls at once with slight variations (different proteins or sauces) so you don't get bored.

Light but Sustaining Meals

Lunch shouldn't leave you sluggish. The goal is balance:

- **Protein** keeps you full.
- **Fiber-rich veggies** stabilize digestion.

- **Healthy fats** fuel the brain and hormones.
- **A touch of sweetness** (like apple slices or berries) prevents afternoon sugar cravings.

This harmony of flavors—sweet, savory, tangy—keeps your taste buds satisfied and reduces the urge to snack on processed foods later.

Flavor Balancing: Sweet, Savory, Tangy

Anti-inflammatory meals shine when flavors are balanced:

- **Sweet:** roasted carrots, sweet potatoes, or berries.
- **Savory:** garlic, mushrooms, grilled meats, or legumes.
- **Tangy:** lemon juice, apple cider vinegar, or pickled vegetables.

Tip: Keep a jar of pickled red onions in the fridge—they instantly brighten any salad, wrap, or bowl.

Lunch as a Healing Pause

Beyond food, think of lunch as a moment to pause and reset your day. Eat slowly. Step away from your desk if possible. Savor the colors, textures, and flavors. This mindful approach not only helps digestion but also reduces stress, which is itself a trigger for inflammation.

By making lunch intentional, you transform it from a rushed necessity into a daily act of self-care—one that keeps inflammation at bay and energy flowing until evening.

Chapter 7

Restorative Dinners

Dinner is more than just the final meal of the day—it's a moment of restoration. After the chaos of work, errands, and responsibilities, dinner offers the chance to gather, slow down, and nourish both body and soul. For anyone healing inflammation, it's also the meal that most directly affects sleep, recovery, and how you feel waking up the next morning.

An anti-inflammatory dinner should be **grounding yet light**, rich in nutrients but not overwhelming. This is where you lean into simple one-pan creations, vibrant stir-fries, reimagined comfort classics, and meals the whole family can enjoy without feeling like they're on a "diet."

One-Pan Meals: Simplicity Meets Healing

Nothing says relief like tossing ingredients onto a single sheet pan or skillet and letting them transform into dinner with minimal effort. These meals reduce stress, dishes, and cooking time—perfect for busy evenings.

- **Sheet-pan salmon with roasted broccoli and lemon wedges.**
- **Chicken and sweet potato bake with rosemary and garlic.**
- **Mediterranean veggie tray:** zucchini, peppers, eggplant, and chickpeas drizzled with olive oil and sprinkled with oregano.

Tip: For deeper flavor, marinate proteins in olive oil, lemon juice, and spices for 30 minutes before baking.

Baked Salmon: A Healing Classic

Salmon is one of the cornerstones of an anti-inflammatory diet. Rich in omega-3 fatty acids, it supports joint health, brain clarity, and hormonal balance. Baking salmon is not only foolproof, but it also retains nutrients without adding unnecessary fats.

- **Simple baked salmon:** brushed with olive oil, garlic, and fresh dill.
- **Asian-inspired glaze:** tamari, ginger, honey, and sesame seeds.
- **Mediterranean twist:** topped with olives, cherry tomatoes, and basil.

Pair with roasted vegetables or a light grain like quinoa for a complete, restorative dinner.

Veggie Stir-Fries: Fast & Flavorful

Stir-fries are the perfect dinner solution when you want something quick, colorful, and deeply nourishing. Use fresh or frozen vegetables, toss in your protein of choice, and coat with an anti-inflammatory sauce.

- **Base vegetables:** broccoli, bok choy, snap peas, bell peppers, mushrooms.
- **Proteins:** shrimp, tofu, chicken strips, or tempeh.
- **Healing sauces:** ginger-garlic tamari, turmeric coconut sauce, or miso-lemon glaze.

Tip: Keep pre-chopped veggies in the fridge for a stir-fry "rescue meal" that's ready in 10 minutes.

Comfort Classics Reimagined

Comfort food doesn't need to be inflammatory. By swapping ingredients, you can still enjoy hearty dishes like curries and stews without guilt.

- **Golden turmeric curry:** chickpeas, spinach, and coconut milk spiced with turmeric and cumin.
- **Hearty lentil stew:** carrots, celery, garlic, and tomatoes simmered in bone broth.
- **Shepherd's pie makeover:** swap mashed potatoes with cauliflower mash, layered over turkey and veggie filling.

These dishes bring coziness and satisfaction while working with your body, not against it.

Family-Friendly Twists

Eating anti-inflammatory doesn't have to mean eating separately from your family. With a few adjustments, you can create dishes that everyone loves:

- **Taco night:** serve grass-fed beef or black beans with lettuce wraps or gluten-free tortillas. Add avocado, salsa, and fresh herbs.
- **Pizza night:** cauliflower crust topped with tomato sauce, roasted veggies, and goat cheese.
- **Spaghetti night:** zucchini noodles or lentil pasta tossed with homemade tomato sauce and turkey meatballs.

Tip: Let kids build their own bowls, tacos, or pizzas with a variety of anti-inflammatory toppings. It makes them part of the process and encourages healthier eating habits.

The Power of Evening Nourishment

The foods you eat at dinner influence how deeply you rest at night and how well your body repairs itself while you sleep. Choose meals that are restorative rather than heavy, and you'll wake up refreshed instead of sluggish.

Remember: dinner is not just about closing the day—it's about setting the stage for tomorrow's health. Each evening plate is a chance to repair, restore, and renew.

Chapter 8

Snacks & Small Bites

Snacking often gets a bad reputation, but the truth is, snacks can be powerful allies in your anti-inflammatory journey—when chosen wisely. The wrong ones (chips, cookies, sugary drinks) fuel the flames of inflammation, drain your energy, and leave you hungrier than before. The right ones, however, provide steady fuel, keep blood sugar balanced, and satisfy cravings without guilt.

Think of snacks as **bridges between meals**—small bites that keep your body nourished and your mind focused. They don't need to be complicated; in fact, the best snacks are often the simplest.

Quick Energy Balls

Energy balls are one of the easiest anti-inflammatory snacks you can make ahead. Packed with fiber, healthy fats, and natural sweetness, they're a perfect afternoon pick-me-up.

- **Base ingredients:** oats, almond butter, chia seeds, flaxseeds.
- **Natural sweeteners:** dates, raw honey, or a touch of maple syrup.
- **Flavor boosts:** cinnamon, cacao powder, coconut flakes, turmeric.

Tip: Roll a batch on Sunday, store in the fridge, and grab 2–3 whenever you need a boost.

Veggie Sticks & Dips

There's nothing more refreshing than crisp vegetables paired with a creamy, flavorful dip. Instead of reaching for chips, reach for crunch that heals.

- **Veggie options:** cucumber, carrots, celery, bell peppers, broccoli florets.
- **Dips:** hummus with extra olive oil, guacamole with lime, tahini-lemon dressing, or white bean garlic dip.

Tip: Pre-cut veggies in jars of water in the fridge. They'll stay crisp for days and be ready to snack on instantly.

Smart Swaps for Chips & Cookies

It's not about giving up the flavors and textures you love—it's about recreating them with ingredients that support healing.

- **Chips** → Kale chips or roasted chickpeas. Seasoned with sea salt, garlic powder, or smoked paprika for crunch.
- **Cookies** → Almond flour cookies sweetened with dates. Rich in protein and low in refined sugar.
- **Candy** → Dark chocolate squares (70% or higher). Packed with antioxidants and deeply satisfying.

These swaps keep the comfort while removing the inflammatory triggers.

Evening Snacks That Don't Spike Inflammation

Evening snacking can be tricky. The wrong foods—like ice cream, chips, or pastries—spike blood sugar and interfere with sleep. The right evening snacks are calming, light, and gentle on digestion.

- **Warm golden milk latte** with turmeric and cinnamon.

- **Apple slices with almond butter** for sweet + protein balance.
- **Chia pudding** with coconut milk and a sprinkle of cinnamon.
- **Herbal tea with a handful of walnuts or pumpkin seeds**.

Tip: If you're often hungry at night, check whether your dinners include enough protein and healthy fats. Balanced evening meals reduce late-night cravings.

The Joy of Small Bites

Snacks are not cheats or guilty pleasures—they're opportunities to nourish yourself between meals. By keeping quick, healing options on hand, you turn moments of hunger into moments of care.

The goal isn't to eat constantly, but to eat **intentionally**. A handful of walnuts, a bowl of berries, or a warm turmeric latte may seem small, but over time these small bites add up to major healing.

Chapter 9

Sweet Healing Treats

Desserts often get framed as guilty pleasures, but they don't have to be. When chosen wisely, sweets can actually be part of your anti-inflammatory lifestyle. The key is rethinking what dessert means—not a sugar overload that spikes blood sugar and stokes inflammation, but gentle, nourishing, gut-friendly treats that leave you satisfied without the crash.

This chapter is about embracing balance. You don't need to eliminate sweetness from your life—you simply need to enjoy it in ways that work with your body, not against it.

Low-Sugar, Gut-Friendly Desserts

The typical dessert—cookies, cakes, ice cream—is often

loaded with refined sugar, white flour, and processed fats. These are exactly the foods that fuel chronic inflammation. But by using natural sweeteners and whole ingredients, you can enjoy something indulgent without the consequences.

- **Natural sweeteners:** raw honey, maple syrup, dates, ripe bananas.
- **Flour alternatives:** almond flour, coconut flour, oat flour.
- **Dairy swaps:** coconut milk, almond yogurt, or cashew cream.

These swaps not only reduce inflammation but also add protein, fiber, and nutrients to your desserts.

Chia Puddings: Small Seeds, Big

Healing

Chia seeds may look tiny, but they are powerhouses of omega-3s, fiber, and antioxidants. When soaked, they form a gel-like pudding that feels indulgent while being deeply healing.

- **Classic chia pudding:** chia seeds, almond milk, vanilla extract, topped with blueberries.
- **Golden chia pudding:** almond milk infused with turmeric, ginger, and cinnamon.
- **Chocolate chia pudding:** cacao powder, coconut milk, and a drizzle of maple syrup.

Tip: Make in jars the night before for an easy grab-and-go dessert or snack.

Baked Apples: Nature's Comfort

Dessert

Few things feel more comforting than a warm baked apple on a cool evening. Apples are naturally sweet, full of fiber, and pair beautifully with anti-inflammatory spices.

- **Simple version:** core apples, stuff with walnuts and cinnamon, bake until tender.
- **Indulgent twist:** drizzle with almond butter and a spoon of coconut yogurt.
- **Gut-friendly boost:** add a sprinkle of flaxseed before baking.

This dessert tastes decadent but is as nourishing as it is satisfying.

Dark Chocolate Recipes: A Sweet

Antioxidant Boost

Dark chocolate (70% cocoa or higher) is rich in flavonoids—plant compounds known to lower inflammation and improve heart health. Unlike milk chocolate, it contains less sugar and more healing power.

- **Chocolate-dipped strawberries:** a classic made healthier with melted dark chocolate.
- **Nut clusters:** walnuts, almonds, and pumpkin seeds coated in a thin layer of melted dark chocolate.
- **Avocado chocolate mousse:** creamy, rich, and naturally sweetened with dates or honey.

Tip: Keep a small bar of 80% dark chocolate at home. A square or two after dinner curbs cravings without overindulgence.

Tips for Satisfying Sweet Cravings

Sweet cravings are natural—our brains are wired to enjoy sugar. The trick is to satisfy them without spiking blood sugar or feeding inflammation.

- **Pair sweet with protein/fat.** Apple slices with almond butter or chia pudding with walnuts keep blood sugar stable.
- **Choose fruit first.** Berries, oranges, or pears provide natural sweetness plus fiber.
- **Hydrate.** Sometimes cravings are a sign of thirst—try lemon water or herbal tea before reaching for dessert.
- **Mindful indulgence.** If you choose to eat a sweeter dessert, savor it slowly. Enjoying a few bites with intention prevents overeating.

The Sweet Side of Healing

Desserts don't need to be about guilt or restriction—they can be about pleasure, balance, and nourishment. By reimagining what a "treat" looks like, you give yourself permission to enjoy sweetness while supporting your body's healing.

When cravings strike, let these recipes and strategies remind you: it is possible to have both joy and health on the same plate.

Chapter 10

Drinks & Tonics

What you sip is just as important as what you eat. Drinks can either fuel inflammation—think sugary sodas, processed juices, and energy drinks—or they can calm, hydrate, and restore your body. In fact, beverages are one of the simplest ways to introduce healing ingredients into your daily routine.

This chapter explores soothing teas, creamy golden milk, refreshing smoothies, mineral-rich water blends, and targeted drinks that support digestion and energy. Each recipe is designed not only to quench your thirst but also to deliver nourishment at a cellular level.

Herbal Teas: Nature's Gentle

Healers

Herbal teas are among the most accessible anti-inflammatory tonics. They're hydrating, caffeine-free (unless you choose green tea), and full of phytonutrients.

- **Ginger tea:** reduces inflammation, supports digestion, and eases nausea.
- **Turmeric tea:** rich in curcumin, helps calm joint pain and swelling.
- **Chamomile tea:** soothes stress, supports sleep, and reduces mild inflammation.
- **Peppermint tea:** cools digestion and relieves bloating.

Tip: Steep fresh herbs like mint, rosemary, or thyme directly in hot water for a fragrant, healing infusion.

Golden Milk: A Cup of Liquid Sunshine

Golden milk is a classic anti-inflammatory drink made with turmeric, warm milk, and spices. Beyond its beautiful color, it's packed with healing power.

- **Base:** almond milk, coconut milk, or oat milk.
- **Core ingredients:** turmeric, black pepper (for absorption), cinnamon, ginger.
- **Optional sweeteners:** a touch of honey or maple syrup.

This warming tonic is perfect in the evening, calming inflammation while preparing your body for restful sleep.

Anti-Inflammatory Smoothies

Smoothies are one of the easiest ways to flood your body

with antioxidants, fiber, and healing fats.

- **Green power smoothie:** spinach, kale, pineapple, chia seeds, and coconut water.
- **Berry blend:** blueberries, strawberries, almond milk, flaxseed, and a touch of cinnamon.
- **Creamy turmeric smoothie:** banana, coconut milk, turmeric, ginger, and vanilla.

Tip: Add a scoop of protein powder (plant-based or whey) to make your smoothie a balanced meal replacement.

Electrolyte Water Blends

Hydration is essential for fighting inflammation, but plain water can sometimes feel dull. By infusing it with minerals and natural flavors, you can transform water into a healing tonic.

- **Lemon-ginger water:** supports digestion and detoxification.

- **Cucumber-mint water:** refreshing and cooling on hot days.
- **Coconut water blend:** mix with lime juice and a pinch of Himalayan salt for natural electrolytes.

Tip: Keep a large pitcher of infused water in your fridge to encourage steady sipping throughout the day.

Drinks for Digestion and Energy

Targeted drinks can help address specific needs—like calming your stomach or lifting your energy naturally.

- **Apple cider vinegar tonic:** warm water with a teaspoon of apple cider vinegar, lemon juice, and honey for gut health.
- **Green matcha latte:** provides gentle caffeine, antioxidants, and steady focus without the crash of coffee.

- **Fennel tea:** reduces bloating and supports healthy digestion.
- **Beet-ginger juice:** energizing, circulation-boosting, and anti-inflammatory.

The Healing Power of Sipping

Small daily rituals—like brewing tea, pouring golden milk, or blending a smoothie—can become anchors of healing in your routine. Drinks are more than hydration; they're a way to pause, nourish, and reset.

Every sip is an opportunity to heal. Choose wisely, and you'll feel the difference not only in your digestion and energy but in your overall sense of balance and vitality.

Chapter 11

Lifestyle Beyond the Plate

Food is powerful medicine, but it isn't the whole story. Healing inflammation requires a holistic approach—what you eat matters deeply, but so does how you sleep, move, and handle stress. In fact, stress, poor rest, and inactivity can undo the benefits of even the most carefully planned diet.

This chapter is about shifting from a diet mindset to a lifestyle—one that weaves healing practices into your daily rhythm so that every choice you make supports your body's natural ability to thrive.

Stress Reduction: The Hidden Key

Chronic stress is one of the most underestimated drivers of

inflammation. When your body is stuck in "fight or flight" mode, stress hormones like cortisol remain elevated, keeping inflammation active. Learning to calm your nervous system is just as important as choosing anti-inflammatory foods.

- **Sleep:** Aim for 7–9 hours per night. A consistent bedtime, cool dark room, and screen-free wind-down routine make a world of difference.
- **Mindfulness:** Daily practices like meditation, breathwork, or even pausing for three slow, deep breaths help regulate stress.
- **Journaling:** Writing down worries before bed or gratitude lists in the morning clears mental clutter.
- **Nature time:** A short walk outdoors reduces cortisol levels and promotes calm.

Tip: Think of rest not as wasted time, but as an active investment in healing.

Gentle Movement & Inflammation

Exercise doesn't have to mean punishing workouts. In fact, high-intensity training done too often can increase inflammation. The best movement for healing is **gentle, consistent, and enjoyable.**

- **Walking:** 20–30 minutes daily improves circulation and joint mobility.
- **Yoga & stretching:** Reduces stress, loosens tight muscles, and supports lymphatic flow.
- **Tai chi or qigong:** Slow, intentional movements that combine exercise with mindfulness.
- **Strength training (moderate):** Builds muscle that supports joints and improves metabolism.

The goal is not to burn calories but to nurture your body into strength, resilience, and balance.

Creating a Sustainable Anti-Inflammatory Lifestyle

The most important step is making this way of living sustainable. Anyone can follow a plan for a week, but true healing happens when you weave these choices into your daily rhythm.

- **Small, steady steps:** Instead of overhauling everything at once, focus on one habit at a time—like swapping soda for infused water or adding a nightly 10-minute stretch.
- **Find joy in the process:** Choose foods, exercises, and routines you actually enjoy. Pleasure and healing can go hand in hand.
- **Community support:** Share meals with loved ones, join a walking group, or invite a friend to yoga. Healing is easier when shared.
- **Flexibility, not perfection:** The goal is consistency, not rigidity. One indulgent meal won't

undo your progress—what matters is the overall pattern of your lifestyle.

When food, rest, movement, and mindfulness come together, you create not just a diet but a way of life that supports long-term vitality.

The Bigger Picture

An anti-inflammatory lifestyle isn't about chasing quick fixes—it's about building a foundation for the future. Imagine waking up with less pain, more energy, clearer focus, and a lighter spirit. That's the gift of living beyond the plate.

Every meal, every breath, every night of rest becomes a chance to reset and restore. And over time, these small daily acts add up to a profound transformation—one where you are not just surviving but thriving.

21-Day Meal Plan (Printable Format)

To make this book not just informative but actionable, here's a simplified **21-Day Meal Plan** you can print, pin to your fridge, or slip into your planner.

Each week follows the phases from Chapter 4:

- **Week 1: Calm Inflammation** – Focus on leafy greens, berries, salmon, olive oil, turmeric, and ginger.

- **Week 2: Heal the Gut & Balance Hormones** – Add probiotic foods (yogurt, sauerkraut, kefir), high-fiber vegetables, flaxseed, and bone broth.

- **Week 3: Energy Restoration** – Combine steady proteins, healthy fats, and complex carbs (quinoa, sweet potatoes, lentils) for lasting energy.

Use the daily meal rhythm (breakfast, lunch, dinner, snack, hydration, movement, journaling) as a structure, then plug in recipes from the book to personalize your reset.

Glossary of Key Terms

Antioxidants – Compounds found in fruits, vegetables, and spices that protect cells from damage.

Chronic Inflammation – Long-term, low-grade inflammation that contributes to disease and fatigue.

Curcumin – The active compound in turmeric known for its anti-inflammatory effects.

Electrolytes – Minerals (like sodium, potassium, magnesium) that regulate hydration and muscle function.

Gut Microbiome – The community of bacteria in your digestive tract that influences immunity, hormones, and digestion.

Omega-3 Fatty Acids – Healthy fats found in salmon, walnuts, and chia seeds that reduce inflammation.

Polyphenols – Plant compounds found in berries, teas, and dark chocolate with healing properties.

21-Day Anti-Inflammatory Meal Plan (Printable Companion)

Each day follows the reset framework: Breakfast → Lunch → Dinner → Snack/Tonic. Hydration (8+ glasses of water or herbal teas) and light movement (20 – 30 minutes walking, yoga, or stretching) are encouraged daily.

Week 1 – Calm Inflammation

Day 1

- **Breakfast:** Blueberry chia smoothie with spinach and almond milk
- **Lunch:** Quinoa salad with roasted veggies and avocado

- **Dinner:** Sheet-pan salmon with broccoli and sweet potatoes
- **Snack:** Energy balls with oats, flaxseed, and almond butter

Day 2

- **Breakfast:** Overnight oats with walnuts, cinnamon, and blueberries
- **Lunch:** Mason jar chickpea salad with tomatoes, cucumbers, and olive oil
- **Dinner:** Golden turmeric curry with chickpeas and spinach
- **Snack:** Sliced apple with almond butter

Day 3

1. **Breakfast:** Veggie scramble with kale, garlic, and turmeric
2. **Lunch:** Lentil soup with carrots and celery

3. **Dinner:** Baked salmon with lemon and herbs, served with roasted zucchini

4. **Snack:** Dark chocolate square with walnuts

Day 4

- **Breakfast:** Green smoothie with kale, pineapple, ginger, and chia seeds
- **Lunch:** Collard green wrap with hummus, peppers, and cucumber
- **Dinner:** Chicken and sweet potato bake with rosemary
- **Snack:** Carrot sticks with tahini dip

Day 5

- **Breakfast:** Golden milk with chia pudding topped with berries
- **Lunch:** Quinoa bowl with avocado, roasted beets, and arugula

- **Dinner:** One-pan cod with roasted bell peppers and olives
- **Snack:** Roasted chickpeas with smoked paprika

Day 6

- **Breakfast:** Warm oats with pumpkin seeds, banana slices, and cinnamon
- **Lunch:** Spinach salad with salmon flakes, lemon vinaigrette, and walnuts
- **Dinner:** Stir-fried broccoli, bok choy, and shrimp in garlic-ginger sauce
- **Snack:** Celery sticks with guacamole

Day 7

- **Breakfast:** Turmeric smoothie with banana, coconut milk, and vanilla
- **Lunch:** Roasted veggie bowl with quinoa and tahini drizzle

- **Dinner:** Lentil stew with garlic, onion, and tomatoes
- **Snack:** Golden milk latte with a handful of almonds

Week 2 – Heal the Gut & Balance Hormones

Day 8

- **Breakfast:** Kefir smoothie with blueberries, flaxseed, and spinach
- **Lunch:** Bone broth soup with zucchini noodles, carrots, and herbs
- **Dinner:** Baked chicken with garlic, lemon, and roasted Brussels sprouts
- **Snack:** Coconut yogurt with chia seeds and cinnamon

Day 9

- **Breakfast:** Overnight oats with chia, almond milk, and raspberries

- **Lunch:** Mediterranean wrap with hummus, arugula, and olives
- **Dinner:** Grilled salmon with roasted asparagus and sweet potato mash
- **Snack:** Cucumber slices with hummus

Day 10

- **Breakfast:** Scrambled eggs with sautéed spinach and onions
- **Lunch:** Lentil and vegetable soup with turmeric
- **Dinner:** Turmeric coconut curry with chickpeas and bell peppers
- **Snack:** Apple slices with walnut butter

Day 11

- **Breakfast:** Green smoothie with kale, pineapple, and ginger
- **Lunch:** Quinoa bowl with avocado, roasted cauliflower, and tahini

- **Dinner:** Baked cod with tomato-basil sauce and sautéed greens
- **Snack:** Dark chocolate avocado mousse

Day 12

- **Breakfast:** Chia pudding with coconut milk and cinnamon
- **Lunch:** Spinach salad with boiled eggs, avocado, and sauerkraut
- **Dinner:** One-pan roasted chicken with carrots and onions
- **Snack:** Herbal tea with walnuts

Day 13

- **Breakfast:** Oats with pumpkin seeds, blueberries, and almond butter
- **Lunch:** Roasted beet and lentil salad with arugula
- **Dinner:** Salmon with ginger-miso glaze, served with broccoli

- **Snack:** Roasted chickpeas with turmeric

Day 14

- **Breakfast:** Kefir with flaxseed and banana
- **Lunch:** Bone broth vegetable soup with garlic and herbs
- **Dinner:** Lentil curry with spinach and coconut milk
- **Snack:** Golden milk latte with a square of dark chocolate

Week 3 – Energy Restoration

Day 15

- **Breakfast:** Green smoothie with spinach, chia, and citrus
- **Lunch:** Mason jar salad with quinoa, chickpeas, and lemon dressing
- **Dinner:** One-pan baked salmon with roasted veggies

- **Snack:** Energy balls rolled in coconut

Day 16

- **Breakfast:** Overnight oats with cinnamon, blueberries, and walnuts
- **Lunch:** Avocado wrap with hummus and sprouts
- **Dinner:** Grilled chicken with roasted sweet potatoes and broccoli
- **Snack:** Herbal tea with roasted pumpkin seeds

Day 17

- **Breakfast:** Scrambled eggs with turmeric, spinach, and onions
- **Lunch:** Lentil and kale soup with garlic
- **Dinner:** Stir-fry with shrimp, bok choy, and bell peppers
- **Snack:** Chia pudding with blueberries

Day 18

- **Breakfast:** Turmeric smoothie with banana and coconut milk
- **Lunch:** Quinoa bowl with avocado, roasted zucchini, and tahini drizzle
- **Dinner:** Golden chickpea curry with spinach and tomatoes
- **Snack:** Dark chocolate nut clusters

Day 19

- **Breakfast:** Kefir with chia, flaxseed, and raspberries
- **Lunch:** Spinach salad with salmon, walnuts, and olive oil
- **Dinner:** One-pan roasted chicken with root vegetables
- **Snack:** Apple slices with almond butter

Day 20

- **Breakfast:** Warm oats with cinnamon, chia, and banana slices
- **Lunch:** Bone broth soup with lentils and roasted carrots
- **Dinner:** Baked cod with Mediterranean herbs and veggies
- **Snack:** Roasted chickpeas with garlic powder

Day 21

- **Breakfast:** Green smoothie with pineapple, kale, and ginger
- **Lunch:** Quinoa bowl with avocado, beets, and chickpeas
- **Dinner:** Salmon with garlic-lemon sauce and sautéed greens
- **Snack:** Golden milk latte with walnuts

Acknowledgment

I wish to thank the countless individuals—readers, health practitioners, and nutrition experts—who have inspired this work. Your questions, insights, and shared experiences shaped this book into something practical and accessible. Above all, I am grateful to the community of everyday people seeking healthier, more energized lives; your determination proves that transformation is always possible.

www.ingramcontent.com/pod-product-compliance
Lightning Source LLC
Chambersburg PA
CBHW030557080526
44585CB00012B/403